Glint & Swerve

Glint & Swerve

Poems by

Veronica Patterson

Cover design by Shay Culligan
Cover image by Sascha Bosshard on Unsplash
Swan image by Qasim bilal on Unsplash
Author photo by Veronica Patterson

ISBN: 979-8-90146-815-9
Library of Congress Control Number: 2026937275

Kelsay Books
502 South 1040 East, A-119
American Fork, Utah 84003
Kelsaybooks.com

More Praise for *Glint & Swerve*

Veronica Patterson's *Glint & Swerve* is a house of many windows, a marvelous study in attention. This work demonstrates how perception shifts across a life, across a moment, across a page, or across a lake. Take hold and hang on. Let yourself rise into the dependable but ever-changing light with these swans.

—Jack Martin, author of *Throwing Hunger: Poems*

More Books by the Author

Full-Length Poetry Collections

Sudden White Fan (Cherry Grove Collections, 2018)
& it had rained (CW Books, 2013)
Thresh & Hold (Big Pencil Press, 2009), Gell Poetry Prize winner and Colorado Book Award Poetry finalist
Swan, What Shores? (NYU Press Poetry Prize, 2000), Academy of American Poets' James Laughlin Award finalist and recipient of Colorado Book Award and Women Writing the West's Willa Award
How to Make a Terrarium (Cleveland State University, 1987)

Prose Poem Chapbooks

Maneuvers: Battle of the Little Bighorn Poems (Finishing Line Press, 2013)
This Is the Strange Part (Pudding House Publications, 2002)

Poetry & Photography

The Bones Remember: A Dialogue (with photographer Ronda Stone)

Acknowledgments

Thank you to the following publications, in which versions of these poems previously appeared:

Atlanta Review (finalist, annual contest): "Inland Passage"
Blue Mountain Review: "The Gold Fish," "Proposal"
Copper Nickel: "Snow Picnic," "From Behind the Mountains"
Crosswinds: "*Knit Me a Loose Scarf of Their Flights,*" "Where Does 'Again' Go?," "Winter Sunday Afternoon"
Dry Creek Review: "The Brothers"
Hole in the Head Review: "Bearings," "Candelabra with Horses," "Carried Away," "Dreaming on the Ides," "For the Pocket Cat," "From the Window at Dusk,"
IMPROV: "Sleeping"
Malahat Review: "Every Year the Elk"
Monserrat Review: "The Orange in the Open"
Natural Bridge: "At the Poetry Appreciation Workshop"
Pratik: "Auguring," "My Grandchild"
Southern Poetry Review: "Walking the Poem," "The Audible"
Spillway: "Seven Swans"
Stone Gathering: "A Charm Against the Language of Politics"
Tar River: "Gravity," "How to Grow a Pencil"
Tupelo Press's The Last Milkweed: "Autumn Is a Honey Locust Tree"

Contents

III. Swerve

IV. Trove

V. Wake

The Blue-Green Stream

Every time I have started for the Yellow Flower River
I have gone down the blue-green stream.

—Wang Wei

Seven Swans

There were seven swans, fresh
from a fairy tale, five white
and two black
but three of them were grieving
and four fog
and six hungry and two
unavailable.
Five were meadows—no—
nettles, and
none of them larks.
One was mine. And another
the bruised world.
They foretold nothing
with certainty. And all
the swans, where the swans
swam, were invisible. Nevertheless,
I relied on the glint
and press of their
absence: the swerve
of neck, the trove
of feathers, the wake.

I. Glint

One Bird on a Branch Opens the Day

especially in late winter. Two
birds twisting close in flight
lean into a future
devising a nest, swift
as spring comes, weaving
a bowl of twig-grass
hope.

Three silhouetted
against feathery clouds,
stop me. Four birth
a cawing band, dressed
in black. (Four-and-twenty
baked in a pie flew out,
singing.)

Five founded
a village in a stubble field
that won't last past furrowing.
Six costumed as leaves
pretend to blow away
and return to bow,
inventing theater.

In Susan Glaspell's *Trifles:*
a strangled canary, a strangled
husband only the women
connect but never tell.
After a Bard enthusiast
brought all Shakespeare's birds
to Central Park, that theater,

some died, sparrows survived,
European starlings *thrived,*
slathering their murmurations
across the country, wreaking
damage. But isn't their name
pretty? Sandhill cranes dance,
exuberantly tossing grassy
confetti. Rising from ponds
in New Mexico, snow geese
pull the sun up. The fact is
only if my lungs fill with air
in borrowed wings of rib, only
then can I speak.

Walking the Poem

Ducks on the pond lift and skim away
from my shore path. Buffleheads.
The Canada geese mutter-honk, mutter-honk,
circling slowly near a small island.
From a rim of cattails and reeds taller than I am,
a hidden great blue heron creaks up eon by eon
and just above the water's surface pterodactyls
to the opposite shore. The gulls' cries, rough
with salt and sand, drag an ocean
into the morning. Water ripples, time
shimmers, and in my bones' marrow
red blood cells stir, the day vast and luminous.

Gravity

At the window facing west,
I gauge the storm's debris—
last leaves, twisted locust pods
spilling seeds, bare branches,
long strips of bark peeled
from the old maple. Squirrels
frenzied in the disordered
too-much. One pauses, erect,
on one end of a curved strip of bark.
Another, leaping from the maple's trunk,
lands on the other end, lifting
the first, which comes down,
whipping the other up,
and for an oddly elastic moment
they jump alternately,
see-sawing. I laugh. True story,
I could add, as we sometimes say,
as if none of the others we told
were. Truth being no more than—
no, released from—
this rib of bark in the littered back yard.
For a moment I see my younger brother
in his torn blue jacket, straddling
a board on one side of a fulcrum, rising
on a playground a thousand miles away,
as the years come down.

How to Grow a Pencil

—after receiving a daughter's gift of novelty pencils

Pencils with seed-
holding gel caps
where erasers
would be (seeds,
the opposite
of erasure).

A card
instructs me
in English
from the Chinese
how to grow
the pencils.

Use at ordinary
times.
But I don't
have any.

Time seems
(*only when pencil*
used can be planted)
of the essence
(*please grow*
within a year).

These
words stop me:
pencil stood the grave wrapped.

I see a tiny mourner
in a cloak
by a matchbox-sized
hole. Boxed in
a corner of
the printed card
are the names: sweet

basil, lucky clover,
mint, lavender,
impatiens. And a last line:
all over the sky   thyme   forget me not.

Skein

I live in a house with many windows,
light structures slats into doors
at the end of wood-grained rivers leading
into another world. Mornings I have

an orange sun. Wind strokes the small lake
until the water wriggles like the coat
of a pleased animal. Inside, waterlight
shimmers across the ceiling. My mind swims.

A mountain range ruffles the horizon, but
steadies me. The thorny branches of the ancient
honey locust tree crackle the sky's glaze,
especially on full moon nights.

When it's warm, bees float through
the catmint, each stem coated with tiny purple
blossoms. One afternoon, bees crisscrossed
the south window like tracer bullets, zooming

dark against light. Then slowly they wrapped
themselves around the base of an old lilac bush,
becoming a single dark skein, and, when I
looked next, were raveling into dusk.

Photograph of a Moment

We're on the shore of the lake
staring at something in the water
or the water itself. My mother

crouches, in a navy jacket, dark pants
and red sandals with gray socks. One
graceful hand is on her right knee. My

older sister, blond hair flying, wears
a light blue sweatshirt; both brothers
wear dark jackets. My long brown

hair, French braided, falls down
a rust-colored jacket. I see
our concentration. The littlest,

a year old, almost disappears, his face
white as light. He holds one palm up.
The next brother, maybe four, angles

one arm behind his head as if to help
him focus. In back of us, tall grass rises
the color of ripe wheat. What

rivets us? Driftwood? A fish?
The rest of our lives? No matter
how hard I stare—nothing

illuminates the coming story. Could
the photographer please back up
or *grow older!* I mean, *come closer!*

The Brothers

—for Howard, Evan, Mark

You see them at family gatherings
after the food is gone
and the football game is over.
They lean forward in chairs
or tip back, feet almost touching,
making angles too strong
to be broken. Laws of physics
do not apply.

They are so private together.
Their laughter cannot be explained,
welling from voices that whispered
bed to bed in the dark.

Solid, they exclude no one:
cousins run between them on missions;
wives circle and drift away.

They stand with a foot on a fence,
shoulder against a doorway,
arm on a car roof. And their father
might join them, next of kin,
aligning his face with theirs.

Time surrounds their geometry.
Leaning, they hold each other up,
talking of sports and other days
and things in general, how they are,
how they are.

Incantation

—for the Old World Rabbits of Ukraine, and their people

Each month begins with rabbits,
rabbit rabbit, shared with my sister
and brother by email, a charm

we learned young to bring luck to each
month. Our mother never said why. Having
lost one brother, these words become

an odd and sturdy bond. The only
pet rabbit we had, among dogs and cats,
a lamb, and a calf, was mean and bit us.

He was named Hassenpfeffer, German
for rabbit stew, and now I seem to
remember—he *did* disappear

suddenly. From our far-flung states
we note the presence of rabbits
in our yards, gardens, and on trails.

Their incandescent ears at sunrise
as I walk east up the alley. No one knows
the exact origins of this centuries-old

lucky-month enchantment, just the rules:
rabbit rabbit must be the first words uttered
on the first day of the month. Sometimes,

here in Colorado, I cheat, saying *rabbit rabbit*
on New York time, the place where I grew up
and learned it. You have to know where

you are, what to say, and exactly when.
Rabbit rabbit. Rabbit. I add a rabbit
for the lost one. All the lost ones.

Where Does "Again" Go?

—for Megan

I watched   wind-curled lake waves
through the window   my hand holding this cup's
sea-green handle   not as slender as
a newborn finger   your birthday
delivered each year   fragile and private
as an old telegram   I will not see
your eyes again   that I saw once just after
birth   that their dark blue was ocean
vortex where a ship unwarned   goes down
and all   I still try to fathom   words
my diving bell   that (again) I will not (again)
see (again) not   that dusky hair, trickle of red,
then breathing   that small body
with faulty circuitry   that only God
the cells confused   and without
instructions   that every day you have
taught me   that the present   that you were
cracks open in no time   all the way back to
eyes ultramarine   which means beyond the sea

The Orange in the Open

On a day without flags or false bottoms
we were headed out to dinner when we saw
on the tar of the parking lot
an orange where it had come to rest
or risen from the vena cava of our longing.
Neither crushed nor venerable, it was round
and good. No grommet in its side declared
it a faker or trap. Was it there
to colonize a world safe for
citrus or to lead rolling expeditions
to trip us into fruition? Irrationally
we saw ourselves joining the Irish Free State
or heading for Odessa on behalf of this tiny sun.
Brighter than iron rust, more
fragrant than hibiscus, quietly it
began to order our hearts'
hierarchy. At the top was the heart's own
expansion, chamber by chamber, room by admitting
room. After that, a concentric ripple
effect came over the Riviera
of our conduct. O we were wildly
civilized by this dimpled Buddha. After dinner,
it was still there, its shadow grown long
as a path. We marveled stoutly and set off
to do surprising good.

At the Poetry Appreciation Workshop

A man comes in late. The rest of us have finished brief introductions, so he is next. He feels he must instruct us at length on Keats, Shelley, Wordsworth, where each died, words that mark those places. But he has a scrap of white paper—Kleenex?—stuck to his nose. Suddenly, I can't hear him. I brush my hand over my own nose surreptitiously, can't look at him. How did that paper get so white? I cough away a bubble of laughter. Where's poetry now? I ask myself. Where are the petals on the wet, black bough? Once I read that any fragment of paper might hold the name of God in Hebrew. We could add his to the 210,000 fragments already in the Cairo Geniza. Or could that shred hold a poem, something briefer than haiku? A *hai,* a *ku?* I convert my chortle to a sneeze and admonish myself. We're all in this together.

II. Press

Surprising the Air

—in the voice of a young woman working
in a southern cotton mill, 1911

We are not slaves, but we are
dust. I came to the mill at ten.
I joined others like me.
When visitors came, the foreman
said we were just bringing our parents
their lunch.

At first I imagined the threads
on the loom becoming
sheets and curtains, shirts
and dresses in a city I might
one day see. I sang to the thump
of looms until the sound

drowned my voice. We are
not slaves, yet we are dust.
Church says so. When the workers
can't breathe, the doctor whispers
"cotton dust." But not to the ones
in charge. Church says

we're dust, but the young man
from the North, who spoke of unions,
said we were sky stuff too. Warm nights
he showed me stars that fell. We lay
down to count the others. He said
so much, then left, not knowing

he would have a daughter. He
wrote once, to say all workers
would rise up. But if I daydream
a better future at the mill, I'll lose
fingers. So I dream nights—*dark is mine*—
next to our sleeping child.

In the letter my fingers have worn soft,
he wrote that he saw too many tired
and hungry faces. I see him
in the small face we made.
He opened my eyes,
but our daughter has his.

We heard about the girls
in the Triangle Waist Factory fire.
No worker here dared speak
of it. How they were locked in,
their choice—to burn or jump.
From nine floors up

they jumped. Sidewalks
were lined with bodies. Only
then were there marches.
They jumped so far down
that others rose up. But how
can I protest when this child
needs food? I'm bound here.

Yet the girls who jumped
keep falling through my dreams,
skirts blooming. In the air
did their eyes open wider
or did they close them, those girls
who surprised the air?
Tell me if—for a moment—
they flew.[1]

---

[1] *On March 25, 1911 in New York City, in the Triangle Waist Factory fire, 146 people died, 123 women, many of them recent immigrants working in poor and dangerous conditions.*

The poem was written in response to "Winnsboro Cotton Mill Blues," by composer Frederic Rzewksi.

I Dream of Taking John Keats to Hear a Western Meadowlark

Western Meadowlark
A clear, whistled introduction, notes followed by
a rapid cascade of bubbling, rich, flutelike notes.

The call liquid: silk ribbon yellow in a mischief breeze~
the silence between calls~ a chasm of ecstasy~ ache of snowmelt
in the canyon~ drift of crabapple blossoms~ quick of the young
fox's run~ still crouch of a rabbit~ curl of joy in Jules Breton's
Song of the Lark~ the young woman's face~ a waking dream

The call liquid: blue scarf loose around my daughter's neck~ a
ripple crossing the lake~ confetti grass tossed by a sandhill crane~

descending the piano's glissando~ night shimmer of moon path
on water~ curve of the humpback whale's flukes~ darkling water
gone~ a line of drowsy bees coming to swarm the old lilac's trunk~
pouring forth tiny souls~ like nightingales tender over the meadow.

The call liquid: This bird's anthem might have healed him.

After the News Came

1. *The First Hour*
Are you sleeping, are you sleeping,
brother Tim? brother Tim?
Morning bells are ringing
Mourning bells are ringing
        ng   ng   ng

2. *The Second Hour*
I remember the story
of a Christmas, when you—
five or six—stayed until closing
in one store, choosing a bell for
your brother and two sisters. You
rang each bell over and over.
How did you know even then
that each of us had a tone
we would keep for life?

3. *The Third Hour*
Yours is the other sleep, the one
we learned of just after
your happy voicemail about
visiting with you in San Diego.
I have kept your message. I'm looking
for my green bell.

The Altar I Will See To

I will see to it that the poker chips
are mother-of-pearl and come from
your father's button factory.

I will see to it that your stories
are retold (how you loved to say, but not
explain, that your sister was your cousin).

Your blond guitar will be tuned, next
to a yo-yo, walking its own dog, coconuts,
chestnuts, palm ivory. I'll see to it.

Your baklava will be made and sent to
my sister and our last brother for the holidays,
with a pen and ink card you drew

when our family was young. I will
see to it that your glass lab beakers
shine, though they might have more

than chemicals. Distilled bathtub
gin. I'll see to it that you're appointed
Keeper of the Eddystone Light.

How we loved that folk song. Our mother
was in fact a mermaid, slick with scales,
our lives still being weighed. The altar cloth

will be your lab coat, on it your bolo tie
and turquoise clasp. She wants to add the white
dress you first saw her in. If you agree,

I'll see to it. Decks of cards for all the bridge
you played won't become our rickety rented
houses, though a metaphor is available.

Everything will gleam in the lit wicks
of your 78 years. I'll light them all
to see how you are still here.

The Gold Fish

—for Tim

In the trunk of the old maple
outside my kitchen window,
many branches lost to wind,
a hollow deepened. Thinking of you
as you entered yet another

recovery program, I found
a gift you had given me,
a stone that fit in my palm.
Swimming beneath
its lacquered surface

a flame-haloed gold fish,
the *betta splendens,* Siamese
fighting fish that drew you
in our childhood aquariums.
Did you love that fish, sensing

a need long before you knew
what your fight would be
before you found glass walls
inside you couldn't break?
After I placed the stone in the hollow,

talisman or prayer, I left it for years.
Then three days after your daughter's
wedding in California, where you were
sober and happy, you died on a San Diego
sidewalk. Heart failure. Back home, I went

to get the dark-shining rock, that golden fish,
but the tree had grown over it. The swelling
had new, lighter bark. A belly
with a navel. This is true but
I don’t know what truth it is.

Self Checkout

One morning a young man in a wheelchair
flew across the ends of aisles, passing

me over and over. Black hair, wild,
ragged shirt: *disheveled?* But he looked

elated. Was he high and on what? In the self
checkout, he grinned and said, "You remind me

of my grandmother. She always sang 'I'll Fly Away.'
Do you know it?" Not thinking, I sang,

and he joined me in his resonant tenor. We grinned
at each other. I finished filling my bag.

Driving home,
I couldn't shake off

those words, that young man, our sudden
connection. I sang it to myself again.

Had his grandmother flown? What
had she meant to him?

I haven't seen him again, but the song plays
him, or is it me? over and over.

Elegy for the Voices Below

—missing, in a year of virus and no travel

Each winter holiday, two voices
murmured below. Back
and forth, back and forth. Sudden
laughter. Counterpoint opinions.
I would come to the top of the stairs,
look through spindles
to the downstairs room. Just as
once I peeked and listened, a child
in pajamas, from a stair landing
to my parents with their friends,
talking, laughing, dancing.
    Two
grown daughters had come
every year from their lives
briefly to this house, talking
feminism, history, movies,
books, gender, theater, music,
remembering their growing
up, bedroom by bedroom, teacher
by teacher, friend by friend, cousin
by cousin. The room's lake
of sound rippled with delight.
    I am
starving for their voices, their
soprano and alto song. The sisters
as only sisters talk. Each year,
after they left, I would find
a few long hairs, light
and dark, to wind around my finger.

To Autumn

—for George Floyd, after rereading John Keats' "To Autumn" in 2020

Season of
when everything hurts. When everything's hurt. The fires shocking, the dry fuel load abundant. Daughters too far away and justice farther. Or further, my English teacher would have said, because it's not actual distance. Or is it? Flames in mountain forests, in the cities, in the soul. Season of mists, John Keats wrote, not meaning smoke.

Conspiring
the maturing sun rises red with warning. What fruits will it fill with ripeness? Apples to be pressed to cider. Hard-pressed to the core, unable to breathe, we find where fear lies. Few peaches this year with their rose-gold scent of *yes*, their plump furred curves. Barred clouds linger above gold fields.

Who Hath Not Seen
arms rise in protest against injustice like stalks of wheat, row upon wave, in streets place after place. We haven't sown justice deep enough to reap. And a virus harvests the careless, the careful, the caring, cutting swaths to stubble across this land, this world, unready hearts. Mourning kin become a wailful choir.

Gathering Swallows
I walk into morning masked and see a green pumpkin pondering change, a zucchini escaped from garden to gutter. Back home, a ripe cantaloupe beckons with its heady scent. Orange thoughts of juice and seeds flood-light my gloom. I make and drink peach tea. On the bottom of the wild-rose painted cup as I rinse it, I see a tiny rose,

Borne Aloft
petals flung wide, blown open, like a heart.

Candelabra with Horses

—remembering Jim Doyle

Wild ducks
fly in every direction
as if a season were lost.

A vacancy
in the cliff dwelling,
an absence in me.

No death requires a coffin
yet ashes confuse the wind,
dry my tongue.

This poem is a postcard
from the dinosaur age
as I remember it.

Tyrannosaurus Rex,
what meteor struck?
I will remember you

each time I see
an orangeade stand
thatched with blackbirds.

Now come horses
shining and deliberate,
carrying candles.

Carried Away

Don't brood.
There is a place
where morning light
knows the throats
of birds
and ten thousand
stirrings in the wood
pause for a bell
ringing in the distance.
Spend an hour gathering
new kindling—
the shadows of branches—
for a different fire.
No one's counting
years. Or storms.
An empty gourd
floats down a sliver
of stream, a silvery
stream, a shivering
stream, and, at the last
minute, toss regrets
aboard, no—leave them
ashore. *You* leap!
The sky will come too.

III. Swerve

From the Window at Dusk

I am not this silence
but in it I hear a strange cry
over and over. Below the window
I see a fox *keening*

I want to say—its cry
that of a child for its
lost mother. Then I see
a coyote pacing up and down

the lake shore at the end of the yard,
their movements parallel.
The fox the coyote might kill
deliberately draws its attention

but why? Is it distracting
the coyote from a den? What
rules that I don't know apply?
Dusk is so lonely I'm lonely

in my deepest root.
When at last the coyote
disappears down the rip-rap
to the lake, the fox

slips behind a screen
of low spruce branches.
I stand and stand. Waiting
for my emptiness to speak.

Elegy Triptych

—for Tim

What I Saw and Heard
March, eucalyptus trees, pale bark peeling. Bougainvillea. Grass green and high. A river flowing in reverse, tide coming in. Valley after valley. Yea though I walk. Tiny green buds that inched away as snails. Other surprising ravines. Gulls wheeling. Slant of last light. From a green hill, sunset over the ocean. Three bay horses. Later, frogs we couldn't see in the dark chorusing loud as a glee club.

some song of the wild
in spring, death coming alive
needing to be fed

I Did Not Know
After the wedding, after I had flown home, the country of ceremony became the country of death. Between them, not so much as a screen door. I had worn the tropical blouse to your ocean. My bags had been full of dress-up clothes and joy infested with memories. Three days later you were found dead on the street. The bride and groom sent photographs, including you, bride-father, but you were gone. Then we—two sisters, one brother—spent hours remembering you as a child, with all the childhood pets—dogs, cats, a rabbit, a calf, a rat, a lamb. Fish. You—funnier than a fish, slipperier than a fish.

you returned to us
for momentary visits
but for how long?

Can We Keep Him?

Though once content with a litter, in which one tumbled over the other, slept in a pile, we invented birth order. Then, job descriptions: first child, in charge; second child, dazzled, but watching; third child, trying everything. Fourth child, *baby*, we said, as he trailed behind us. He who dragged home pets, pleading, “Can we keep it?” wanting some breathing thing lower in the order, to lean against his leg in times of need. We left home in the same order—one, two, and three—each with a story to launch us. He stayed the longest, under the influence. Though he married, began a new birth order, full of love, guess what?

he got away   love
doesn’t fix everything
we couldn’t keep him

The Audible

the slight crackle when a match lights
and the spit-scratch of the candlewick igniting,
the sound of a snowball I brought in
to melt in the sink, one crystal's minute collapse
after another, the light ratchet of the belted kingfisher's
cry. Thin as a pin drop, the nick of change coming.

But what I mean is the click of one pinecone scale
opening to its seed. And I also mean
the unscripted ticking of that green cone,
which I set on the counter in the kitchen,
how all the scales popped wide in the warmth,
each seed fierce—Is there a ting
when a soul quickens?

Bearings

—for E

I love moments of half-dark before sunrise
as the year turns inward

the house with you asleep
and my <u>hold</u> rippling outward

to daughters in their places, sister,
brothers who began with me

drinking milk and running into the world
until night came with its Milky Way

*

and in the mountains six days ago
with my sister and one brother

I saw the Way again and the Big
Dipper on the horizon ready

to one day scoop us up
and I was—we were—shiny, and earth

turned beneath us, injured but just-then asleep,
dreaming Himalayas

*

and sometimes I know the other dark by
its scald in my throat, as when we just left

the hospital room where your brother lay, gauze
twisted high above his opened head,

a Trojan soldier crumpled after battle,
I murmured, go back in to him,

say good-bye before we leave—
and then you knew too and you did

Take It or Leave It

walking by the river
three days after snow
and freezing cold that helps
tamp mountain fires

a morning of sun and still—
gold leaves on just enough
trees, the river running
loud and clear

I see frozen in edges
of icy snow
a black backpack
next to a picnic shelter

and a new black jacket
still in its plastic package
I could chip them free
looking around, no one

anywhere near but
the river, its banks, where
homeless people often camp
no one

should I take them
somewhere to be given
again, or leave them
so that someone returning

might be relieved to see
the small heap of black
and black, a crumpled story
only the water hears

Buddy Holly, Sing On

Every day
at our two bathroom sinks
we sing in the cool morning
slipping vertically through the window,
mountains serene to the west—
or mountains *there* and their reflection
in the lake serene. One sheer canyon
wall holds sunup, no—
it's your face.

It's so easy
to sing the loud misery
of the Winter Dance Party tour,
songs Buddy belts now
to the blue spruce, grebes diving,
and, if we raise the volume,
to a great blue heron
on the shore, a slender fox
by the den. We sing back-up.

It's a little closer
October 2001. We wail
his song about fools, the ones
who look back at us from
the bathroom mirror
as the harvest moon slips down
morning and we prepare for a day still
choked with the Twin Towers' ruin,
bumping hips, as usual, but more

That'll be the day
awake.

From Behind the Mountains

Even when wind bursts from mountains and lakes,
the garden east of the house is not disturbed,
blue love-in-the-mist and sturdy tansenium. Slender

blades of Japanese iris tilt and lie down, but only
because spring falls back to the rhizome.
In the wind, the pots on the west-facing deck

rock in clay saucers, as inside, you read
by the fireplace, the rustle of pages entering
the pine branches, catlike, pawing the house,

the lake beyond the window frothing, all of it
washes over me, cleaning me for a joy so intense
that even the least bearable days, weighted

with our *missing*—fathers, mothers, friends,
are not to be mourned.
They inhabit their own clarity.

The wind steadies, falls, the lake lulls.
The path is no clearer, but the mountains beckon
boots out of the closet.

Inland Passage

—to Alaska

we entered fjords through sudden
openings between looming stone walls.
In round inflated Zodiacs we skirted
pale blue icebergs. It was late April.

We crossed a bay, where humpbacked
whales rose and dove, rose
and dove, their curved tails catching
the last gild of sun.

When we came to the glacier,
the ship stopping an exact specified
distance from this sky-cliff of ice,
it calved a high-rise that collapsed

and shattered the water. Shocked,
we cheered from the deck, yet
the fractured glacier shuddered
inside our bodies, a silent crack

as the mammoth white bone
splintered, and in a Costa Rican
rainforest, we did not see the canopy
slit, admitting too much light

for what's below to live.

Voice

Do you have an elephant in your house?
Do you have a serpent in your throat?
No, I do not have a serpent in my throat,
shedding skin after skin, that slight rasp.

Do two men lean in through the walls
of your throat? No, the fine hairs on the back
of their wrists do not catch the sun.
Do you have an elephant in your throat?

No, I do not have her swaying in the house.
Do you have Ariadne in your throat? No,
she cannot spin thread strong enough to hold
the elephant that is not in my house.

No, she will not balance on two legs for you.
Do the floors wrinkle with light? No. Though
my tongue flicks between two Ithacas, the past
won't darken the whole future of my throat.

With no elephant in your gray-sided house,
does her stark, buried eye shine wild above it?
Do you have an elephant in your house?
No, fortunately, I have an elephant in my throat.

Knit Me a Loose Scarf of Their Flights

It is the swallows
that console me, their interwoven
swooping, bringing insects home.
Arc upon arc, they etch morning.

Their nests console me. A sudden
village of mud huts burgeons under the bridge
overhang, each a thousand pellets,
and in this gypsy encampment, hatchlings

poke tiny wide-open beaks into a river
of air. They will be fed. Flights
crisscross above the river,
an emulsion of swallows, birds, air

and insects, immiscible, yet this exact mix
consoles me. Are they swift flecks
of eternity? I'm not sure why I ask
that question, and that, too, consoles me.

IV. Trove

Every Year the Elk

October. Snow curtains
the silent meadow
shutting us in where the young bulls
rear against each other
and the bugles rise, fall, break
at the end into pieces.

In the car, we drink steaming coffee,
then walk a back road, spot another band,
dark shapes at dusk, believed
as much as seen. We match strides
but say nothing. When one bugle
ends in a squeak, we laugh.

As we leave, I catch movement.
You stop the car. Twelve elk
pour across the road, heads turned
to our lights, leaping. Seconds later,
when we reach the place
where land drops away, no sign. Gone

they are ours.
Vanishing into the dark,
they run through us, a ribbon of elk,
twisted once and forever,
crossing my mind into yours,
yours into mine, breeding

the old wonder.

For the Pocket Cat

—for Lucretia, named after suffragist Lucretia Mott

For the pocket cat, who could hide in a teacup.

For she whose long hair, even puffed, could not reach the edges of
her being.

For her face was divided by color but never her loyalty.

For she chose a person and saw her through. And vice versa,
rescued and rescuing.

For she helped with writing, though she herself preferred to sit on
the pages.

For she was wise early and taught her companion by batting the
pens.

For she ate little, for she was only half in this world. For she slept
light as sun on every sill.

For in her first life she was a small cloud and in her second life
a falcon, her heart an opal.

For no one knew her true beginning, nor which life she was on,
which is to say *cat.*

For she was tri-colored, sprightly, and whole. For her purr was
the motor of a world.

Three Moons

This One
Spring, our family
camping. My sister
and I cross a moonlit
just-plowed field in silence
toward the murmur of water,
the glittering silver
stream we glimpse
in the distance.
Each dark furrow is combed
by light. Then we see
small clods move. No—
we're stepping on a carpet
of tiny new toads
leaping into the air.
For a long moment
we can't move.

Above the Small Lake
the moon floats down
to serrated mountains.
Slowly? Quickly?—
yes, and that path
of light over water,
with its pluck
of departure and
arrival, narrows.
A path I still want to walk.

By the Open Window
5:30 am. What startled
my sleep, I ask
the small lake, then
follow a glimmering wake
to a pale apricot
moon descending
at the speed of
ripening fruit.
I blink. I am
a blink. Still
how lucky
to be up early
in the longing.

Snow Picnic

—ghazal for E

Dead relatives flock to the picnic. They keep their calendars swept
clear of snow,
events, everything. The sky has served this feast; not a single ant
dots the snow.

I'll pack a basket with ample drifts, keep everything chilled. We'll
break icy twigs
for forks. So much room at the table, on long, long benches
cushioned with snow.

We'll picnic on just one delicacy, whipped to peaks, the bitter pain
folded
in and sweetened now. But what sad confectioner would add this
flourish of snow?

All those who left suddenly, before dinner, must be hungry for us
by now:
my mother first, then yours, our fathers, and the child who slipped
into early snow.

Geese flying overhead, wanting to spell *home,* form the first letter
of my name.
I wouldn't swallow winter, but I'm still famished for earth. Then
let it—

The First Time I Ate Nasturtiums

Walking in summer rain
in a mountain town
at night with a woman,

a poet I had just met,
not ducking into doorways
or under overhangs,

but letting cool drops
wash who we were
from our faces. We began

to pick nasturtiums
from window boxes
along the street, popping

them onto our tongues. Each
leaf was a tiny green plate
and the blossoms brought

back orange and yellow
snapdragons from childhood
whose mouths I squeezed

open. But it was our mouths
opening to this traveling
salad. To the peppery

taste, the tonic, the bite.
Through the shimmering wet
window of one lighted room,

we saw music on a stand and
a man conducting thin air. His
precise baton let us guess notes

and words and sing in the rain.

My Grandchild

Walk into the time that is coming
—Jane Hirshfield

Last night, climbing the stairs
from the basement
to read and maybe sleep
despite the sick ache of a world
that cannot breathe,
I came face to face with a rabbit
at the glass back door. Like
images in the virus news, this
could be a grandchild visiting
a grandmother, a thick pane
between them. We looked long.
I have no grandchild
but there you were.

I have books I could read to you:
Peter Rabbit, The Country Bunny
and the Little Gold Shoes, Watership
Down when you're older, that book
of a world destroyed, flight, courage,
mistakes, change, rebuilding.
"Rabbit rabbit," I say first thing on
the first day of each month,
a childhood ritual for luck.

There are foxes here, I want
to tell you, a large hawk. I can't
protect you. Is the world
weakening? Darkening? Let's
go softly now to curl in separate

sleeps. I'll dream how to act on
our behalf, for the sake of this earth,
on which our kin may still thrive when
you and I are gone. I touch the glass
and your ears twitch forward.
I ask, What time is it? for you,
for me, this place, this planet.

Winter Sunday Afternoon

Tiny beads of snow pick at the window
like a clock ticking. On a card table, my father
is measuring, cutting, and taping triangles to make
a hexahexaflexagon from long instructions
in an issue of *Scientific American.* I've finished
my geometry homework, but soon he'll look up,
see that I'm done, and show me how to complete

these proofs in fewer steps, his thoughts igniting
mine. He finishes the complex cootie catcher—
origami fortune teller—and shows me its process.
He loves every calculated challenge and risk—chess,
marriage, poker, children, bridge, biochemistry,
racing a car. I don't think to ask him why he plays
this 3-D math game. I don't think to ask about

his biochemical research. I don't think to ask him
about anything. He is my father. After he died,
I found an old newspaper article on a new cancer
treatment; in the photograph, he holds up to light
the contents of a test tube. In the years I knew
his focus was chemical nutrients for growing
crops faster—rice in the Philippines, not on all

7,641 islands, but in multiple elsewheres. Later,
inside his glass beakers, in his lab, in his white lab
coat, in him, had the chemicals changed? He left
Ithaca and deep snows for a company in San Diego
to head research and development. What had stalled
in cold silence or drawn him to warmth, ocean,
a different future? I know nothing.

Outside, that Sunday afternoon, no two alike, softer
snowflakes begin to fall and melt like, or into, dreams.

Light Switch

"Nothing's queer," said the Virginian, "except marriage and lightning."
—*The Virginian*

the way in predawn dark
my fingers slip up a light switch
I need to flip down for *on.* I want
everything to be clearer—up for *on*
down for *off,* no matter which way
I enter or leave the room. But
the world changes, I change, light
changes every day

and the way I learn you new
now after half a century. I see, for
example, we're both workers by nature,
not vacationers, though we travel a little
and love everything we see. Yet when
light in Alaska lingered past 11 pm
you finally went to bed—a tiny bed
on a small ship. I stayed on deck until
I could no longer see the bright-edged
tail of the last humpback whale

and the way the edge of a spoon
holds light. Yesterday you told me
how you stack the clean spoons
when you put them away in the drawer,
lifting those already in the spoon slot
to the top, like T-shirts in a drawer
that might wear out if you wore
the same ones over and over. Metal
spoons? I ask, seeing again who you are,
I am, how distinct and oddly radiant
our uses of order and light.

Did he not love us as much as he loved the world?

—to Ralph, childhood collie

Puppy who came with our youngest brother, baby and dog tugging and chewing on two ends of a stick. You grew faster. Full grown collie with selective hearing, you who only came when you felt called. Who, when we lived in town, found each of us wherever we were—in school, in the woods, on campus. Who came home from fields on the edge of town muddy, your coat matted with burs or ripe with skunk, your nose a bouquet of porcupine quills. One rainy night you came home in a taxi at 1:00 a.m.; my sister witnessed it from her window. The taxi turned into the driveway, the driver emerged and then let you out of the back seat. O, Ralph, you who won an obedience class for being the only dog who didn't run from your "stay" when a dogfight erupted. Ralph, you were the big-eared Buddha who knew when to listen, who taught us life's rhythm of obey and disobey, who understood when departure was required and how to return as needed in any available vehicle. Where is the fierce yellow taxi that will bring you back?[2]

---

[2] *My sister saw Ralph's arrival, but she was sick and running a fever—no one believed her. Years later, my father encountered the owner of a popular downtown bar, the man who, when Ralph kept slipping in whenever the door was opened and shook wide showers of water over customers, sent Ralph home in a taxi.*

Proposal

Let's do all the things
that don't matter
now: canoe on quiet mornings
when the lake is still, find

the new restaurant
in town and try it
before it closes. Let's
hold hands. Then you do

one thing, and I'll
do another so we
can return. Let's be
fragile together. Let's

hike the trail
to the cascade
along torrents of green
frothy water. The world

is a worse mess than
when we first thought
we could fix it. Storms
are predicted for later,

rain, lightning, possible
flooding. You get
the paddles and life
jackets. Let's *wake*

our bold promise—
I mean, let's *take our old*
thermos. We'll go
forth, then float, drink

coffee, tell each
other stories.
This is a binding
contract. Sign here.

V. Wake

Sleeping

—after Neruda, for Evan

Sleeping, you are young as your first suck,
limp with trust, sure as a bud on its branch.
Your cheekbone catches daybreak.
Sleeping, you return to first principles, uncurling.

Sleeping, you are small as your first word
and as large. You were awaited, delighted in. Plum
from a slender tree, you have always known *ripe.*

Sleeping, you are a path dreaming of feet,
pollen and nightwind in your hair.
Sleeping, you are steady as a lichened boulder,
calm as sun

as if—coming feet first, leaping the first hurdle
of your unfolding—you kicked gladly free of the womb
in assurance of milk.

A Charm Against the Language of Politics

Say over and over the names of things,
the clean nouns: weeping birch, bloodstone, tanager,
Banshee damask rose. Read field guides, atlases,
gravestones. At the store, bless each apple
by kind: McIntosh, Winesap, Delicious, Jonathan.
Enunciate the vegetables and herbs: okra, calendula.

Go deeper into the terms of some small landscape:
spiders, for example. After a speech compromising
the environment on behalf of some technology,
recite the tough, silky structure of webs:
tropical stick, ladder web, mesh web, filmy dome, funnel,
trap door. Chant the spiders: comb footed, round headed,
garden cross, feather legged, ogre faced, black widow.

Remember that most short verbs are ethical: hatch, grow,
spin, trap, eat. Dig deep, pronounce clearly, pull the words
in over your head. Hole up
for the duration.

Dreaming on the Ides

"What sayst thou to me now? Speak once again."
—William Shakespeare, *Julius Caesar*

The dream opens in a room of dusky light,
evening coming on. Two young men
seem familiar with each other.

I am there, watching. An old guitar lies
on a low table. Dark wood, scratched,
gouged splinters of wood missing.

My father arrives in a Hawaiian shirt.
Not looking at us, he picks up the guitar.
Foot on the table, he plays, his blunt

freckled fingers flying. The shivering
riffs of jazz, pluck and slap of flamenco,
thrum of folk songs in dimming light.

The young men nod at each other,
lean forward. They are not my brothers.
My father, yes, who died suddenly

on the Ides of March. At early spring dinners
growing up, we intoned "Beware the Ides
of March," and laughed. A campfire ignites

on the shore of Cayuga Lake, guitar music carries
over water and circles back into the dream. Dad,
how shall I wake further?

Auguring

1.
An absence in the shape of a catalpa tree at the corner of Lake and Garfield. In spring, frothy branches scattered small orchids I picked up and brought home in my palm to float in a small crystal bowl.

Who else remembers? It burned one night, flames rising, swallowing bark. One side charred onyx. But the next year it bloomed. And the next, died.

2.
There *had been* a catalpa tree—what rusty tense is that? Past perfect? Now I know why once-upon-a-time was invented.

Heart-shaped leaves the size of plates. Frilly blossoms, throat and tongue, mouth open for an aria. Inside, veiny purple tracks to follow.

From the Muscogee word *kutuhlpa,* for its winged seeds, white, fringed at both ends, from a long bean-like pod, green in spring, brown in fall.

3.
A school bus stopped at that corner. One Fall when I walked by, every hole in the perforated metal pole that held a stop sign had a brown pod skewered through it until it seemed an instrument of torture. Was it the waiting schoolkids who devised that?

4.
The sky is empty right there, no rustling, no hum of bees. Nothing has replaced the tree. But somewhere, has a seed flown, landed, and wormed its way into dirt, burrowed deep, auguring a future?

Autumn Is a Honey Locust Tree

—for Evan

If autumn is a honey locust tree, and it is,
then winter is each bared-branch threshold of the sky.
The tree shades us in summer. Grief is

the lake behind the house. & contentment is a sentinel—
the great blue heron that gathers gulls and egrets
to pooled fish. But not us. The once-born child, a gamin

who loved the world, as she did—its blue wild geranium
blossoms, is still named Megan. Her brief dark hair
sprouted fragile hope. & her hours become a book

crusted with salt. I spend years walking every
morning and returning to you. To her. We canoe
on the happy gleam of lake, paddling, as we do,

gently. We litany the names of mountains to the west.
Sometimes we, and we do, hold each other & feel
three hearts beat. When lakeshore appears in fall

we descend the rip-rap to skip flat rocks two or three
or seven times, each a sinking dream. We are
learning to watch the ripples, which never exactly end.

My Himalayas

When I'm asked about the necklace,
a figured silver cylinder on a chain, I say
It's a Tibetan prayer wheel.

Then comes, *Did you travel to Tibet?*
No, I answer, it's not a souvenir
but a remembering.

I found it on Navy Pier in Chicago,
walking with my daughter. She had
just performed at the Children's Museum,

a one-woman play we wrote together—
Susan B. Anthony as a young school teacher.
After, one young man marched off

into other exhibits chanting, "Votes for Women!
Votes for Women!" In a restaurant in California,
for another daughter's graduation,

a woman serving me spoke to me in Tibetan.
I shook my head, but asked if there were
a prayer inside. Yes, she said, smiling.

And I knew then I would turn
and turn the wheel to send prayers
for my daughters, one ghost, two flesh,

my family, the place I live, the place you live,
concentric circles of street, city, state, country,
earth. For grass, trees, mountains, gorges,

for water, for water, for water and air.

From the highest region in the world, this
wheel touches the highest region inside, where
the heart is a sturdy yak in my Himalayas.

Chrysalis

—how can I keep from singing?

in my hand is a jar emptied of all
but a segment of dried milkweed stalk

and curled leaves. Two hours earlier,
it was brilliantly stained glass

in black and orange, as if some small god
had been trapped in a sanctuary

~

when I took the jar from the garage shelf,
where I had forgotten the chrysalis

brought home from the field,
for my daughters to learn from,

I set it on grass, unscrewed the lid,
and leaped back. Slowly, a live thing

unfolded each wing, clung stunned
to the rim, then floated away

~

above my lamentation. Waking from
another sleep, I saw how I would be

astonished over and over, lucky
my whole life, finding islands of light

on the dark borders of such wings

October Leaf Still Curled on My Desk in February

—for E

All its small veins form a watershed. You pulled it from a branch I couldn't reach as we contemplated the tree's 48-year-old height and width. Buildings have spread around it. No one will miss this leaf. But sometimes we still imagine *might have.* At home, a slight draft rasps the leaf along my desk. I can't smell it, can't smell that day. A crack runs from edge to stem. Flame-shaped tips won't ignite. Curled, it casts shadows briefly like wings. Sprung from a low branch of what only we call Megan's tree, given by your parents in her memory as we grieved.

the tree didn't stop
rings of flood and drought, She-Who-
Almost-Unfurled   I—

My Mother's Voice

Walking down a street
with my husband, two daughters,
and visiting relatives to a restaurant:
my aunt, eight years younger
than my mother, her husband,
daughter. I'm behind her,
talking to someone, laughing.

Suddenly, my aunt stops.
Turns. "You have your mother's
voice." For a moment her sister
was back. Our faces open
into different stories, then
slowly close. The mother
I tried to never be,

then dead three years.
I recall her voice most
clearly in piercing words
I had blotted out. An alcoholic
intent on dying as our daughters
entered the world. And yet
I was shaken. Shaking.

When your heart failed
did we cry out?

Decades later, one of my
vocal cords paralyzed in heart
surgery, I'm thinking again. Her

life began mine; did it also save
me? I don’t know, but
I’m listening. What
will I sing now in our voice?

Cloud Forest

This hour I tell things in confidence
I might not tell everybody but I will tell you.
—Walt Whitman

I think that the manatee, pale gray, curved, floating beneath the
water's surface, is an ocean cloud

And that a wedding dress is a billowing cloud with a veil of rain

And fungus white in the damp woods is an earth cloud and I do not
care if it is edible or poisonous

And white dog-tooth violets make tiny clouds that ruffle the garden

And each white swan, gliding, each pelican spiraling, each white
egret doubled in the water-mirror is a feathered cloud

Cotton bursting soft from its boll and pillows stuffed plump with
down are clouds from which the mist of dreams rises

And the full moon is the bright sister of clouds and they sing
together and I join them

When the moon is new, I walk the cloud-trail of the Milky Way
and spirits are with me

A cocoon is a cloud to hold and empty life, unraveled to weave a
shroud

And milkweed seeds—cumulus clouds in a satin canoe

Consider how bones hold clouds of flesh, and the soul a cirrus
cloud shimmering above the body

And sheep a herd of woolly altocumulus, and lambs skinny clouds
gamboling

And the great white lenticular whale swims in turning pages

Walt Whitman's beard and Albert Einstein's hair are cirrus clouds
full of lightning

For every poem and every book is a cloud of knowing
and unknowing

And love a cloud that passeth misunderstanding and life is great
as death

The Most Beautiful Morning in the History of the World

Cool, with a slight breeze, but it's not just that.
Leaves quivering a green sheen into the sunrise,
        but it's not just that.
Lake rippling a glossy blue, ticking in my ears,
        but it's not just that either.
Mountains with threads and tiny knots of snow,
        but not only that—
a small golden dragonfly on the sidewalk, dead, perfect,
        its translucent wings. Could it be the center?
The gingko tree's small fans wave from a sixth-grade
        reading comprehension test: "Gingko Tree:
        The Living Fossil."
Tomatoes' greeny-blush on vines, zucchinis hide, apples
        hum, pears pull down branches canny-sweet.
For just a moment, no news from elsewhere (war, starvation,
        floods, quakes). Clouds move east, piling & stretching.
I'm on the move too, walking, breathing, absorbing, sucking
        it all in-in-in. But it's not just that. *Tomorrow* doesn't
        exist. I photograph nothing on my cell phone.
My eyes are a camera.

The Readers Ponder My Advice

Should they go north, where some
of the poems point, to classical firs,
a useful austerity, where they could learn
how to build and bank a fire, how to
edit the heart?

Or south, where long oval leaves
hang over a pool into which everyone
jumps naked, later eating ripe mangoes
on striped towels, learning
the skin lessons.

Right now, my words assure them
they won't fall from the earth. They don't
believe in edges or endings. They decide
to leave in October, a Thursday, at dusk,
in shafts of chilly light, walking.

I begin to write them a benediction:
That they have honorable difficulties,
mornings to wake into, children born
through the walls of their heart, a salt sea
of sweet grief.

I decide not to include what could happen
later. I call the new poem "Map."

Whereabouts of the Black Umbrellas

We are . . . our own umbrellas and our own suns.
—John Donne, letter, 1651

Even in the absence of rain
and Impressionist paintings
of wet streets, I know
their silky privacy, see
them

one left behind on an island
near Seattle, where
it forgot to rain,
in the tiny New York
apartment at the top
of narrow stairs
in China Town,
where we ate
Renato's paella and it
stopped raining.
Left behind in
Ithaca, Ann Arbor, Chicago,
Colorado, Asheville,
Alaska, New Zealand . . .

They have marked
place and time, body
and story, each a black
parachute that dropped
me deeper
into this world.

One day
I’ll see them, my flock
of dark suns,
returning—

Keys in a Bowl

I have a key to a small lake.
And a key to clouds: cumulus, stratus, nimbus, lenticular.
I have a key to silence, though when I walk, small birds
insist on threading their trills through air—wrens,
chickadees, finches.
And keys to every rock I brought from Ithaca, which include flat
ones I skipped, and stones laced with curious fossils. Here,
in the West, I have snow-bereted mountains.
I have a key to a metal box, where I stored every little vow,
some full of thoughts I planned to use.
One key opens all the tall blue volumes of the Oxford English
Dictionary, an ocean of words, a sky of words.
A tiny key to a wood jewelry box I never lock, and one
to a suitcase I never fill.
Keys to every tree by leaf and bark and branch, and to shaped
spaces between branches. Each key to a ponderosa pine
smells like butterscotch.
Most keys gleam with mountain ridges, a lake, a ditch, a road.
One gold key on a chain.
How can I unlock time? Unlock new words? Some electric-
hallelujah. A glacier-scraped finger of lake far east of here
might open my past,
but what about our future?

About the Author

Veronica Patterson is a Phi Beta Kappa graduate of Cornell University, the University of Michigan, the University of Northern Colorado, and the Warren Wilson College MFA program in poetry. She has authored eight previous poetry collections and chapbooks, many of which have won awards. Her poems have appeared in numerous publications including *The Southern Poetry Review, The Midwest Quarterly, Prairie Schooner,* and *Spillway*. Patterson has been awarded artists' residencies at the Ucross Foundation, Rocky Mountain National Park, Hedgebrook, the Ragdale Foundation, and the Gell Center. She's also received two Individual Artist's Fellowships from the Colorado Council on the Arts. Her poems have been nominated for a Pushcart Prize, and her essay "Comfort Me with Apples" was selected as a Notable Essay of the Year.

www.ingramcontent.com/pod-product-compliance
Lightning Source LLC
LaVergne TN
LVHW090531110826
845146LV00003B/1057

* 9 7 9 8 9 0 1 4 6 8 1 5 9 *